# ALASTAIR LITTLE

*Lunches*

*Photography by* SIMON WHEELER

THE MASTER CHEFS
WEIDENFELD & NICOLSON
LONDON

ALASTAIR LITTLE taught himself to cook and opened his own eponymous restaurant in London's Soho in 1985. His second restaurant, Alastair Little Lancaster Road, opened early in 1996 in Notting Hill. In the summer he also runs La Cacciata cookery school in Orvieto, Italy.

He has co-authored two books with Richard Whittington: *Keep It Simple*, which won the Glenfiddich Food Book of the Year Award in 1994, and *Food of the Sun* (1995). They also contribute a column to the *Daily Mail* on Saturdays. Alastair Little has made a number of television appearances: on BBC-TV's *The Good Food Show* and *Ready Steady Cook!*, among others.

# CONTENTS

The discovery of a new

dish does more for the

happiness of mankind than

the discovery of a star.

# INTRODUCTION

I spend several months a year at my cookery school in Orvieto. The Bricapo family, who own the estate on which the school is situated, frequently invite me to lunch and although the food is delicious and the company charming, it is still a struggle to wade through three courses, including pasta, at lunch time. Modern work schedules and busy lives demand quicker, simpler food: carbohydrates like pasta, vitamins from salad, tastiness without heaviness.

The following ten dishes are all designed to provide this kind of lunch. One course, with good bread to accompany and a judicious quantity of wine or a beer or two, followed by seasonal fruit and protein-rich cheese.

Some of these are more substantial lunches than others; more calories are needed in winter. I make no apology for the fact that some of the recipes are quite time-consuming, though much can be done in advance: if you want to cook you have to devote a little time to it; if you merely want fast food, go to a fast-food chain.

Alastair

# FARO
## (Mixed bean and barley soup)

250 G/9 OZ BARLEY, SOAKED IN
  PLENTY OF LIGHTLY SALTED
  WATER FOR SEVERAL HOURS
1 x 400 G/14 OZ CAN OF
  BORLOTTI BEANS
1 x 400 G/14 OZ CAN OF
  CANNELLINI BEANS
1 x 400 G/14 OZ CAN OF
  CHICKPEAS
EXTRA VIRGIN OLIVE OIL
2 GARLIC CLOVES, FINELY CHOPPED
2 SPRIGS OF ROSEMARY, LEAVES
  STRIPPED OFF THE TWIGS
1 x 400 G/14 OZ CAN OF CHOPPED
  TOMATOES
SALT AND PEPPER

### BRUSCHETTA (OPTIONAL)
2 SLICES OF GOOD-QUALITY
  COARSE WHITE BREAD
  (PREFERABLY A DAY OR TWO
  OLD) PER PERSON
1 GARLIC CLOVE PER PERSON,
  HALVED
EXTRA VIRGIN OLIVE OIL

**SERVES 6–8**

During soaking, the barley will swell considerably. Transfer the swollen barley to a large saucepan and add 2 litres/3½ pints water. Simmer gently for 1 hour.

Meanwhile, open the cans of beans and chickpeas, drain and mix them together. Rinse the mixture very thoroughly in cold water to rid them of the viscous liquid from the tins. Add the beans to the saucepan with the barley and simmer for 15 minutes.

Pour 4 tablespoons olive oil into a large saucepan, place over a low heat and add the garlic and rosemary; leave to infuse for 5–10 minutes, then add the tomatoes and finally the beans and barley.

Simmer for a further 30 minutes, adding a little more water if it becomes really solid – although this is how most Tuscan soups are served. Season to taste and serve in soup plates. Offer more olive oil to add at the table.

For the bruschetta, toast the bread, rub each slice with a cut garlic clove and drizzle with oil. Eat while hot.

# TAGLIATELLE WITH SOY SAUCE
## and mustard

2 TABLESPOONS JAPANESE SOY
  SAUCE
1 TABLESPOON ENGLISH MUSTARD
  POWDER, MIXED WITH
  1 TABLESPOON WATER
2 TABLESPOONS SUNFLOWER OIL
1 BUNCH OF SPRING ONIONS,
  CUT INTO 1 CM/½ INCH
  DIAGONAL SLICES
COOKED CHICKEN BREAST, SKINNED
  AND DICED (OPTIONAL)
400 G/14 OZ GOOD-QUALITY EGG
  TAGLIATELLE

## TO GARNISH (OPTIONAL)
FRESH CORIANDER LEAVES
FRESH RED CHILLI, FINELY
  SHREDDED
FRESH GINGER, FINELY SHREDDED

**SERVES 4**

Put 4 litres/7 pints water into a
large saucepan, salt it very lightly
and bring to the boil. Mix the soy
sauce and mustard together in a
small bowl. Heat the oil in a large
frying pan over a low heat and
gently cook the spring onions until
soft, together with the diced
chicken, if using.

When you are ready to eat,
drop the pasta into the boiling
water and cook for 1½–2 minutes
or until *al dente* (just tender, but
remaining firm to the bite). Drain
the pasta, reserving 4 tablespoons
of the cooking water, and tip the
pasta into the frying pan with the
spring onions. Add the soy and
mustard mixture, turn up the heat
and toss thoroughly. If the pasta is
not coated with the dressing, add a
little of the reserved water. Serve at
once, with coriander, chilli and/or
ginger scattered over if you like.

# PRAWN SALAD
## *with taramasalata dressing*

40 TIGER PRAWNS (ABOUT 1 KG/
    2¼ LB), HEADLESS BUT WITH
    SHELLS ON
1 GARLIC CLOVE, FINELY CHOPPED
1 LARGE FRESH RED CHILLI, SEEDED
    AND FINELY CHOPPED
SALT AND PEPPER
EXTRA VIRGIN OLIVE OIL
24 RIPE CHERRY TOMATOES
ABOUT 8 LARGE HANDFULS OF
    MIXED SALAD LEAVES
1 BUNCH OF CHIVES, SNIPPED INTO
    1 CM/½ INCH LENGTHS

## TARAMASALATA DRESSING

2 TABLESPOONS GOOD-QUALITY
    TARAMASALATA
JUICE OF 1 LEMON
6 TABLESPOONS EXTRA VIRGIN
    OLIVE OIL

**SERVES 4**

Peel the prawns and slit along their backs to devein them. Continue cutting until the prawns are nearly in two parts and then press them flat to butterfly them. Place them in the grill pan and scatter with the garlic and chilli. Season with salt and drizzle on a little oil. Rub gently into the prawns and ensure that the chilli is evenly distributed. Heat the grill, but don't begin to cook the prawns until everything else is ready.

Cut the tomatoes in half, season and drizzle with olive oil. Wash and spin-dry the salad.

To make the dressing, put the taramasalata in a bowl, whisk in the lemon juice, and then gradually whisk in the oil.

Put the prawns under the hot grill for 2–3 minutes or until they change colour, becoming opaque. They may need turning, but they must not overcook.

Meanwhile, dress the salad leaves and pile on to four plates. Arrange the prawns and tomatoes around the edge of the salad and scatter with chives.

# TOMATO AND MUSTARD TARTS
*with Cheddar cheese and thyme*

250 G/9 OZ PUFF PASTRY
SALT AND PEPPER
8 RIPE PLUM TOMATOES, SKINNED
    AND THINLY SLICED
4 TABLESPOONS DIJON MUSTARD
250 G/9 OZ MILD CHEDDAR
    CHEESE, THINLY SLICED
A LITTLE FRESH THYME
EXTRA VIRGIN OLIVE OIL

**SERVES 4**

Preheat the oven to 180°C/
350°F/Gas Mark 4 and lightly
butter a baking sheet. On a lightly
floured surface, roll out the puff
pastry fairly thinly and cut out four
circles, about 10 cm/4 inches in
diameter. Transfer these upside
down to the baking sheet.

Season the tomato slices
generously. Spread 1 teaspoon of
the mustard on each pastry circle,
leaving a 5 mm/¼ inch border.
Arrange a circle of overlapping
tomato and cheese slices on top,
again leaving the border
uncovered. Arrange more cheese
and tomato slices to fill the centres.
Sprinkle the tarts with thyme and
drizzle lightly with olive oil.

Using the back of a knife blade,
feather the edges of the pastry,
pushing up the borders to form a
low wall.

Bake for 10 minutes or until
the pastry has risen. Reduce the
oven temperature to 160°C/
325°F/Gas Mark 3 and bake for a
further 10 minutes. Serve
immediately, with a green salad.

# ONE-POT DUCK
*with noodles and greens*

4 DUCK LEGS, WELL SEASONED WITH
   COARSELY GROUND PEPPER AND
   SEA SALT
4 TEASPOONS SUNFLOWER OIL
2 LITRES/3½ PINTS CHICKEN STOCK
   (STOCK CUBES DILUTED WITH
   TWICE AS MUCH WATER AS
   STATED ON PACKET)
2 GARLIC CLOVES
2 CM/¾ INCH PIECE OF FRESH
   GINGER, SLICED
8 SPRING ONIONS, CUT INTO
   1 CM/½ INCH LENGTHS (SAVE
   TRIMMINGS FOR THE STOCK)
400 G/14 OZ WINTER OR SPRING
   GREENS, TRIMMED AND
   DESTALKED
8 TABLESPOONS SOY SAUCE, PLUS
   EXTRA, TO TASTE
200 G/7 OZ CHINESE WHEAT
   NOODLES (CHOW MEIN)
A LITTLE SESAME OIL
SOY SAUCE AND CHINESE CHILLI OIL
   TO SERVE AS DIPS

**SERVES 4**

Sauté the duck legs, skin side down, in a little sunflower oil over a medium heat; cook for 30 minutes, then turn and cook on the other side for 20 minutes. Pour off any excess fat. (The fat can be saved and used for sautéing potatoes.) Bring the stock to the boil, adding the garlic, ginger and spring onion trimmings. Bring a large saucepan of salted water to the boil and blanch the greens for 3 minutes. Drain and refresh in cold water. When cool, drain again, squeeze dry and chop coarsely.

Preheat the oven to its highest setting. Strain the stock into a large saucepan and bring to the boil. Add the duck legs and soy sauce, reduce the heat and simmer the duck for 10 minutes.

Take a casserole or four individual lidded claypots (available from Oriental shops) and place the noodles in the bottom. Scatter with the spring onions and the greens. Sprinkle with sesame oil and a little soy sauce. Add the duck legs and pour over the boiling stock. Cover and bake in the very hot oven for 15 minutes. Serve from the casserole or claypot, removing the hot lids carefully.

Soy and chilli oil can be served in dipping bowls.

# SUPREME OF BRILL
## *with mussels and spinach*

1 KG/2¼ LB MUSSELS, CLEANED
   (PAGE 30)
250 ML/8 FL OZ DRY WHITE WINE
1 KG/2¼ LB SPINACH
A LITTLE UNSALTED BUTTER
4 FILLETS OF BRILL (OR HALIBUT
   OR TURBOT), ABOUT 800 G/
   1¾ LB – YOU WILL PROBABLY
   HAVE TO BUY A 1.5 KG/3 LB
   BRILL AND ASK YOUR
   FISHMONGER TO FILLET IT
200 ML/7 FL OZ DOUBLE CREAM
PINCH OF SAFFRON
SALT AND PEPPER

**SERVES 4**

Put the mussels in a large saucepan
with the wine over a high heat. As
soon as the shells open, tip the
mussels into a colander over a bowl
to catch the cooking liquid. Strain
the liquid through a fine sieve into
a clean pan and place over a high
heat to boil until reduced by half.
Leave to cool. Shell the mussels
and place in a bowl with a little of
the cooking liquid; keep chilled.

Wash the spinach, boil for 1
minute, then refresh in cold water,
drain and squeeze dry. Preheat the
oven to 180°C/350°F/Gas Mark 4.

Butter a gratin dish and arrange
the spinach in the dish to form a
bed for the brill. Dot the fish with
more butter, cover loosely with foil
and bake for 12–15 minutes or
until the fish is opaque.

While the brill is cooking, add
the cream to the reduced mussel
liquid. Bring back to the boil and
simmer until slightly thickened.
Add the saffron and season to taste.
When the brill is nearly cooked,
add the mussels to the sauce and
heat through gently. Pour over the
fish and serve from the gratin dish.

# BAKED COD
## *with potato crust*

2 BAKING POTATOES, PEELED

SALT AND PEPPER

4 COD FILLET STEAKS WITH SKIN,
ABOUT 250 G/9 OZ EACH
(FROZEN ONES FROM THE
SUPERMARKET ARE GENERALLY
EXCELLENT)

A PLATE OF SEASONED FLOUR

100 G/3½ OZ UNSALTED BUTTER

2 LEMONS, HALVED

**SERVES 4**

Preheat the oven to its highest
setting. Butter a baking sheet. Slice
the potatoes as thinly as possible,
rinse thoroughly, then dry with
paper towels.

Season the fish on the flesh side
and arrange the potato slices on
this side, overlapping like scales.
Season the potatoes and, using a
fish slice, carefully transfer the fish
to the seasoned flour, skin side
down. Flour on the skin side only,
then equally carefully transfer to
the buttered baking sheet. Dot the
potato scales with small pieces of
butter, then place in the oven and
bake for 15 minutes.

Meanwhile, heat the grill (if
you have a dual-function oven
simply switch from oven to grill
function). Finish browning and
crisping the potato under the grill.

Very carefully transfer the fish
to four serving plates, pour over
any buttery juices and serve a half
lemon on each plate. A simple
green vegetable such as sugar snap
peas would be an ideal companion.

# PORK DIJONNAISE

800 G/1¾ LB PORK FILLET

SALT AND PEPPER

SUNFLOWER OIL

UNSALTED BUTTER

1 GLASS OF DRY WHITE WINE

200 ML/7 FL OZ DOUBLE CREAM

4 TABLESPOONS DIJON MUSTARD

A SMALL HANDFUL OF FLAT-LEAF
    PARSLEY, CHOPPED

A FEW CAPERS OR CHOPPED
    GHERKINS (OPTIONAL)

**SERVES 4**

Cut the pork into 1 cm/½ inch slices, then flatten out into escalopes using a meat bat or rolling pin. Season with a little salt and pepper.

Heat a large frying pan over a medium heat. Add a little oil and a generous knob of butter and cook the escalopes for 4–5 minutes on each side. Do not overcrowd the pan; you will almost certainly need to cook the pork in two batches. When it is done, remove from the pan to a plate and keep warm in a very low oven.

Add the wine to the pan and increase the heat. Boil until the wine has reduced by at least half, then add the cream and bring back to the boil until lightly thickened. Stir in the mustard and parsley, and a few capers or chopped gherkins if you like, then taste and adjust the seasoning. Return the pork escalopes and any collected meat juices to the sauce and swirl until coated. Do not boil the pork in the sauce or it will toughen. Serve at once, with garlicky green beans.

# SAUSAGE AND BEAN CASSEROLE

2 X 400 G/14 OZ CANS OF
    CANNELLINI BEANS, DRAINED
    AND RINSED
1 X 400 G/14 OZ CAN OF CHOPPED
    TOMATOES
EXTRA VIRGIN OLIVE OIL
250 ML/8 FL OZ CHICKEN STOCK
    (MADE WITH A STOCK CUBE)
2 SPRIGS OF ROSEMARY
3 GARLIC CLOVES, FINELY CHOPPED
2 BAY LEAVES
600 G/1¼ LB SPICY ITALIAN-STYLE
    SAUSAGES (OR TOULOUSE
    SAUSAGES)
100 G/3½ OZ STREAKY BACON, CUT
    INTO THICK STRIPS (LARDONS)
400 G/14 OZ MORTADELLA
    SAUSAGE, SKINNED AND CUT
    INTO 1 CM/½ INCH CUBES
200 G/7 OZ FRESH BREADCRUMBS

**SERVES 4**

Preheat the oven to 160°C/
325°F/Gas Mark 3.

Put the beans and tomatoes in
a saucepan with a good dash of
olive oil and place over a medium
heat. Add the stock, rosemary, garlic
and bay leaves and simmer for
10–15 minutes.

Place a large frying pan over a
medium heat, add a little oil and
brown the sausages for a few
minutes, then add the bacon and
mortadella and cook for 2 minutes.

Tip the bean mixture into the
frying pan and return to a simmer.
Taste and adjust the seasoning and
transfer to a wide casserole. Cover
with a thin crust of breadcrumbs,
moisten with olive oil and bake for
1 hour, occasionally adding a few
breadcrumbs or a drizzle of oil as
the crust develops. Serve straight
from the casserole.

# ROAST MARINATED CHICKEN
*with bitter leaves*

2 SHALLOTS OR 1 RED ONION,
  COARSELY CHOPPED
6 TABLESPOONS DIJON MUSTARD
A LARGE HANDFUL OF FLAT-LEAF
  PARSLEY
2 GARLIC CLOVES
JUICE OF 1–2 LEMONS
6 TABLESPOONS OLIVE OIL
10 CHICKEN THIGHS (OR MORE)
A SELECTION OF BITTER SALAD
  LEAVES (CURLY ENDIVE,
  CHICORY/BELGIAN ENDIVE,
  TREVISO, RADICCHIO, ROCKET,
  PUNTARELLA, DANDELION)
2 LEMONS, HALVED

## SALAD DRESSING

1 TABLESPOON SHERRY VINEGAR
SALT AND PEPPER
3 TABLESPOONS OLIVE OIL
1 TABLESPOON WALNUT OIL

**SERVES 4**

Begin making this dish the day before you want to serve it. Place the shallots or onion, mustard, parsley, peeled garlic, lemon juice and olive oil in a food processor and process until chopped and amalgamated. Marinate the chicken thighs in this mixture overnight.

The next day, preheat the oven to its highest setting. Place the chicken thighs, skin side up, on the rack in your roasting tin, having allowed any excess marinade to drop off. Roast for 40 minutes or until well browned and the thigh bones are starting to protrude, an indication that the meat is cooked.

Ten minutes before the chicken is ready, assemble the salad dressing ingredients in a large bowl and dress the salad.

Transfer the chicken to four serving plates and sprinkle generously with sea salt and coarsely ground black pepper. Add the salad and half a lemon. The ideal accompaniment would be a plate of French fries.

# THE BASICS

If you have a reasonably well-stocked larder and refrigerator a satisfying and healthy lunch can be made from sandwiches. Good bread with a few slices of salami or some leftover roast meat or chicken, accompanied by a tomato salad and followed by some tasty cheese is the sort of lunch I often enjoy.

It is always a good idea to put a kettle of water on to boil as soon as you get into the kitchen. It is sure to be useful, whether it is to cook pasta, dissolve a stock cube or blanch vegetables.

## SALADS

Try to find an interesting mixture of salad leaves. The mixed packets sold in supermarkets are often limp after their compulsory washing and sorting.

Although salads should never be left sitting in their dressing, you can get ahead by making the dressing in the serving bowl, and having the salad leaves cleaned and ready. To serve, add the salad leaves to the bowl and toss delicately.

## BLANCHING AND REFRESHING

Green vegetables, such as cabbage and spinach, and roots such as carrots, are often blanched in advance of the final cooking of a dish. This means that they will cook more quickly and evenly at the final stage, and also fixes the colour and texture. To blanch, plunge them into of plenty of salted boiling water for a minute or two, or slightly longer for root vegetables.

Refresh them in lots of cold water, so the temperature is immediately reduced, but do not leave refreshed vegetables sitting in the cold water, or they will become soggy and flavourless; drain them as soon as they are cold.

## TOMATOES

To be sure that you have ripe, tasty tomatoes, try to buy them several days ahead and ripen them on a plate in your kitchen.

Blanching is used to loosen the skin of tomatoes so that it is easy to remove. First cut a cross in the base of each tomato, then plunge into a saucepan or bowl of boiling water. After about 20 seconds, transfer them to a bowl of very cold water; the skin should now peel off readily.

## CLEANING MUSSELS

Wash the mussels in several changes of clean cold water, scrubbing or scraping off loose grit, seaweed and barnacles. Pull out the 'beards' – the filaments of seaweed-like thread by which the mussels attach themselves to the rocks – and discard any mussels with broken shells and any that are open and remain so when tapped sharply.

# THE MASTER CHEFS

**SOUPS**
ARABELLA BOXER

**MEZE, TAPAS AND ANTIPASTI**
AGLAIA KREMEZI

**PASTA SAUCES**
GORDON RAMSAY

**RISOTTO**
MICHELE SCICOLONE

**SALADS**
CLARE CONNERY

**MEDITERRANEAN**
ANTONY WORRALL THOMPSON

**VEGETABLES**
PAUL GAYLER

**LUNCHES**
ALASTAIR LITTLE

**COOKING FOR TWO**
RICHARD OLNEY

**FISH**
RICK STEIN

**CHICKEN**
BRUNO LOUBET

**SUPPERS**
VALENTINA HARRIS

**THE MAIN COURSE**
ROGER VERGÉ

**ROASTS**
JANEEN SARLIN

**WILD FOOD**
ROWLEY LEIGH

**PACIFIC**
JILL DUPLEIX

**CURRIES**
PAT CHAPMAN

**HOT AND SPICY**
PAUL AND JEANNE RANKIN

**THAI**
JACKI PASSMORE

**CHINESE**
YAN-KIT SO

**VEGETARIAN**
KAREN LEE

**DESSERTS**
MICHEL ROUX

**CAKES**
CAROLE WALTER

**COOKIES**
ELINOR KLIVANS

# THE MASTER CHEFS

Text © copyright 1996 Alastair Little

Alastair Little has asserted his right to be
identified as the Author of this Work.

Photographs © copyright 1996 Simon Wheeler

First published in 1996 by
WEIDENFELD & NICOLSON
THE ORION PUBLISHING GROUP
ORION HOUSE
5 UPPER ST MARTIN'S LANE
LONDON WC2H 9EA

British Library Cataloguing-in-Publication data
A catalogue record for this book is available
from the British Library.

ISBN 0 297 83636 6

DESIGNED BY THE SENATE
EDITOR MAGGIE RAMSAY
FOOD STYLIST JOY DAVIES
ASSISTANT KATY HOLDER